D0580010

21st
Century
Skills Library

ROAD TO RECOVERY

GRAY BAT

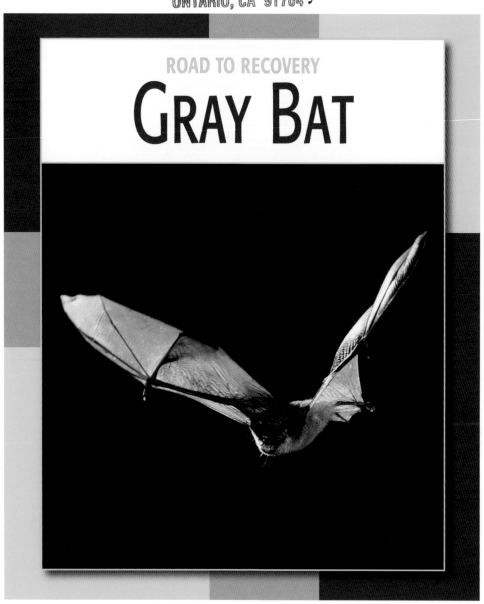

Susan H. Gray

Cherry Lake Publishing
Ann Arbor, Michigan

Published in the United States of America by Cherry Lake Publishing
Ann Arbor, MI
www.cherrylakepublishing.com

Content Adviser: Dr. Brock Fenton, Professor and Chair, Department of Biology,
University of Western Ontario, London, Ontario, Canada

Photo Credits: Cover and pages 1, 4, 5, 6, 7, 8, 11, 12, 14, 16, 20, 24, 25, 26, and 28,
Photos courtesy of Bat Conservation International

Map by XNR Productions, Inc.

Library of Congress Cataloging-in-Publication Data
Gray, Susan Heinrichs.
Gray bat / by Susan H. Gray.
    p. cm.—(The road to recovery)
ISBN-13: 978-1-60279-037-7 (hardcover)
ISBN-10: 1-60279-037-X (hardcover)
1. Gray bat. I. Title. II. Series.
QL737.C595G73 2007
599.4—dc22   2007004445

*Cherry Lake Publishing would like to acknowledge the work of
The Partnership for 21st Century Skills.
Please visit www.21stcenturyskills.org for more information.*

TABLE OF CONTENTS

CHAPTER ONE

FINDING MOM

A group of young bats crowds together.

Mother bats and their babies crowd together on the cave ceiling. The

babies are only about four weeks old, and some are just learning to fly.

They drop from the ceiling and begin to flap wildly. They fly a short way

from the colony, then return.

Dr. Merlin Tuttle, the founder of Bat Conservation International, photographs a bat.

"I soon joined high school friends in exploring . . . caves, quite unaware of the potential harm that could result to bats," wrote Merlin Tuttle about his teenage years. Today, Dr. Tuttle is a famous expert on gray bats. He has spent his life studying and protecting them.

In 1982, Dr. Tuttle started Bat Conservation International (BCI) to encourage other people to help bats. Under his leadership, 14,000 people in 70 countries have become members of BCI. Their efforts have saved millions of bats and educated millions of people.

During the year, the fur of gray bats turns from gray to reddish brown. The bats shed this fur in the summer. The new fur underneath is dark gray. After the summer ends, the fur grows thicker and turns color again. Why do you think the gray bat's fur changes color?

Upon landing, each little bat struggles to find its mother. It doesn't take long. Every mother knows the sound and smell of her own baby.

Gray bats shed their fur in the summer.
The new fur is dark gray.

CHAPTER TWO

THE LIFE OF THE GRAY BAT

Gray bats have long, delicate bones that support their wings.

Gray bats are small mammals. Most adults weigh between 0.3 and 0.4 ounces

(8.5 and 11.3 grams). This is about the same weight as three or four grapes.

From wing tip to wing tip, they measure 10 to 11 inches (25 to 28 centimeters).

Long, delicate arm, finger, and hand bones support the wings.

*Gray bats are active at night. Echolocation allows them
to fly in the dark without bumping into objects.*

Like other bats, gray bats roost upside down. They hang by little claws on their back feet. They also sleep in this upside-down position.

Gray bats are nocturnal, meaning they become active at night. To "see" their way in the dark, they use echolocation. They send out pulses of sound waves from their open mouths. The sounds echo off nearby objects and bounce back. The bat listens to the echoes, compares them to its original sounds, and uses the difference to detect objects. Many bats, including gray bats, also use echolocation to "see" their insect prey.

Gray bats live in caves throughout the southeastern United States. They have winter caves and summer caves. They do not live in barns, attics, trees, or abandoned buildings.

During the winter, they hibernate. Before cold weather sets in, the bats eat a lot and fatten up. They are storing energy for their long hibernation.

Then the gray bats select their winter cave. They prefer caves with large rooms that trap the air. Almost all gray bats go to just a few winter caves in Tennessee, Missouri, Kentucky, Alabama, and Arkansas.

Males and females fly into these caves by the thousands. They find toeholds that will last them through the winter. They crowd together, covering the ceilings of the large rooms. They stay there until spring.

During late March, the bats come out of hibernation. They fly out of their caves and start searching for food. Soon the bats begin moving to their summer caves.

Summer caves are several degrees warmer than winter caves. They are also fairly close to rivers or lakes, where gray bats find most of their food. They fly above the surface of the water and catch flying insects.

Bats crowd together when they hibernate.

Gray bats belong to the largest family of bats—the vesper bats. The word *vesper* comes from the Latin word for "evening." Why do you think this word would be used to describe bats?

If you said because bats are most active in the evening, you are right. There are more than 300 kinds of vesper bats. They are found almost everywhere in the world.

Mexican free-tailed bats emerge from Bracken Cave in Texas. Like gray bats, these bats live mostly in caves and feed on insects.

Many bats find summer caves close to their winter caves. But some travel more than 200 miles (322 kilometers) to their summer homes. On the way to distant caves, bats will rest at "stopover" caves.

Once they reach their summer caves, the bats split up. Males and young bats go to bachelor caves. Adult females go to maternity caves, where they give birth. Each has only one baby. At first, the babies are helpless and cling to their mothers. But they develop quickly. After about a month, they are flying.

Throughout the summer, young and old bats begin to fatten up. In the fall, they head again to the winter caves. If all goes well, this cycle will repeat itself many times. Gray bats can live to be 15 years old.

Learning & Innovation Skills

In the winter caves, thousands of bats pack together in clusters. In a cluster, more than 1,000 bats might be packed into a space the size of a beach towel! Can you think of some reasons why bats would pack together in clusters?

BATS DROPPING AND BAT DROPPINGS

A gray bat perches on a cave wall. The right cave environment is critical for a gray bat's survival.

Gray bats are picky about the type of caves they like. The caves must

have just the right temperature. Winter caves must have large rooms.

Summer caves must be near water. A good cave must be free of visitors

and disturbances.

Over the years, though, some of those perfect caves have been ruined. Some have had too many visitors and explorers. Some have been flooded and are now under water.

The problems began many years ago. During the American Civil War, people searched caves for bat droppings, or guano. The guano was used to make gunpowder. As the war dragged on, more and more caves were disturbed.

Bats that are awakened during hibernation can become weak or die. This is because they burn extra energy when they wake up. Their heartbeat and breathing speed up. They burn up too much of the fat stored in their bodies. A gray bat's body is quite small. During hibernation, it does not have much energy to spare. Too many disturbances during the winter can cause it to starve to death.

Researchers check a pile of bat guano in a cave in Kentucky.

Bats that are bothered in their summer caves are no better off. Females in the maternity caves will startle easily and drop their babies.

Throughout the Civil War, people scoured both winter and summer caves for guano. Gray bats died by the thousands. In time, the war ended and the guano collecting dropped off. Amazingly, the bat populations recovered.

The disturbances did not end, however. Natural events such as cave-ins happened from time to time. People who feared bats tried to kill them or wreck their homes. Cave explorers unknowingly caused bats to die.

The creation of new lakes also hurt the bats. As populations in the southeastern states grew, the need for water also grew. To meet the need, the government created many new lakes. To create a lake, workers would build a huge dam on a river. The dam held back water, letting it rise and

Gray bats help keep the insect population under control. The bats go out at night, visiting nearby lakes, ponds, rivers, and streams. They fly about 16 feet (5 meters) above the water, snagging their prey.

To find an insect, a gray bat uses echolocation. Then it quickly grabs the prey and swallows it. Gray bats eat moths, flies, beetles, dragonflies, grasshoppers, mosquitoes, and wasps. One bat can eat as many as 3,000 insects each night! What do you think would happen to the insect populations if there were no more gray bats?

The bats themselves often become food for other animals. Hawks and owls sometimes feed on gray bats. So do skunks, foxes, and snakes. Usually, it is the slow or sickly bats that are caught.

spread out over a large area. As the water rose, it covered old homes, roads, fields, and caves. Some of those caves were favorites of the gray bats.

Pollution is another problem. The bats are big insect-eaters. Over the years, many streams have become polluted. Some of them contain insect poison that has trickled down from croplands. As streams became polluted, insects could no longer live there. Gray bats could not find enough food. And the insects they did eat often contained poison.

In the 1970s, bat watchers noticed that the numbers were dropping. By 1976, there may have been only 2 million bats left. That year, the U.S. government said the gray bat was **endangered**.

Disturbances can harm a hibernating gray bat. If a bat awakens and moves around, it can burn more energy than it took a month to store. It is important that people act responsibly to keep from harming bats. How can you help keep bats safe?

Poison sprayed to protect crops pollutes streams where insects live. As a result, gray bats can't find enough insects for food.

CHAPTER FOUR

GOING TO BAT FOR THE BATS

Bat researchers carefully examine caves to find out more about bats and ways to help them survive.

After the gray bat became endangered, people came together to help it.

Government workers and scientists met and made a plan. They figured out

the best ways to help the gray bats recover.

They knew they had to protect the gray bats' caves. One way to do this was for the government to buy the land where the caves were. So, the government bought land in several places. Signs went up to warn visitors. New fences and gates kept visitors out. Forests around the caves were also protected. The trees provided safe resting places for the bats.

Scientists began to educate the public about gray bats. They wrote papers about the bat and talked to school groups. They explained why it was important to save the bat and how bats help control insect populations.

Things slowly began to improve. However, problems did come up. One problem involved the

21st Century Content

In 1973, the U.S. Congress passed the Endangered Species Act (ESA). It forbids any government organization, corporation, or citizen from harming endangered animals. It also protects their habitats.

The ESA protects a species only if it has been officially listed as "threatened" or "endangered." Citizens like you can ask the government to include an animal on the list.

Owls are predators of the bat.

gates at cave entrances. Gates were good at keeping people out. However, some gates became clogged with leaves and blocked the airflow through the cave. Some gates did not allow the bats to fly through easily. Some even provided spots for **predators** to perch and wait for bats! Now scientists are designing better gates.

It took a while for the gray bat numbers to rise. There were about 2 million gray bats in the late 1970s. In 1982, gray bat numbers dropped to 1.6 million. By 1992, they were down again. But then things began to turn around. Today, there are about 2.3 million gray bats.

Learning & Innovation Skills

Thousands of gray bats roosting together can actually raise the temperature inside a cave. Why do you think the temperature goes up when bats roost together?

CHAPTER FIVE

GRAY BATS TODAY

Gray bats were put on the endangered species list in 1976.

Gray bats were listed as endangered in 1976. They are still endangered,

but a lot has happened since 1976. The bat population is slowly growing.

This gray bat is injured and unlikely to survive.

Clusters of gray bats cling to a cave wall as a researcher checks on them.

Now, people know a lot more about the gray bat. They know where its

favorite caves are. They have figured out how to protect those caves.

Some people are not happy that bats are getting all this help. They

want to visit caves and see the bats. Some are afraid of bats and want them killed. Others think that saving bats is not worth the trouble. They do not know about the millions of insects the gray bats eat.

Fortunately, many other people are interested in the gray bat. They hope that one day it will no longer

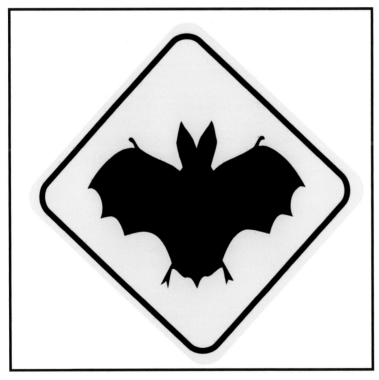

This crossing sign helps protect bats and their environment.

More gray bats hibernate in Alabama's Fern Cave than anywhere else in the United States. The bats start arriving in the fall. By November, more than 1 million gray bats are clinging to the cave ceilings. The U.S. Fish and Wildlife Service owns the cave. No one can enter without special permission.

The U.S. Fish and Wildlife Service is a special unit of the government. It plays an important role in protecting gray bats and other wildlife. To learn more about the work it does, visit www.fws.gov.

Many states have organizations called bat working groups. These groups bring together different organizations and citizens to pursue one goal: helping bats. They do this by studying bats, teaching the public about bats, and urging the government to protect bats.

Bat working groups help people who care about bats to meet and learn from each other. By working together, they achieve a lot.

Gray bat numbers are increasing, but people need to continue their efforts to protect them.

be endangered. When most caves are well protected and bat numbers rise year after year, the gray bat will be out of danger.

Progress has been slow for the gray bat. But today, things are looking better than they have in years.

This map shows where the gray bat lives in the United States.

GLOSSARY

bachelor (BATCH-uh-lur) related to males that have no mates

colony (KOL-uh-nee) a group of animals that live together

echolocation (EK-oh-loh-KAY-shun) a way to detect objects by bouncing sounds off them

endangered (en-DAYN-jurd) in danger of dying out completely

guano (GWAH-no) bat droppings

habitats (HAB-ih-tatz) the natural homes of plants and animals

hibernate (HY-bur-nayt) to become inactive (and appear to be asleep) by slowing down all life processes

mammals (MA-muhlz) animals that have hair or fur and bear live young

maternity (muh-TUR-nih-tee) having to do with motherhood

nocturnal (nok-TUR-nuhl) active during the night

predators (PREH-duh-turz) animals that hunt and eat other animals

prey (PRAY) animals that are eaten by other animals

roost (ROOST) to settle down for rest or sleep

FOR MORE INFORMATION

Books

Graham, Gary L., and Fiona A. Reid (illustrator) *Bats of the World.*
New York: St. Martin's Press, 2001.

Sway, Marlene. *Bats: Mammals That Fly.* Danbury, CT: Franklin Watts, 1999.

Theodorou, Rod. *Gray Bat.* Chicago: Heinemann Library, 2001.

Web Sites

Bat Conservation International
batcon.org/home/default.asp
To read about this organization devoted to conservation, education,
and research involving bats and the ecosystems they serve

The Nature Conservancy: Hubbard's Cave
www.nature.org/wherewework/northamerica/states/
tennessee/preserves/art10128.html
For information on one of the largest protected gray bat colonies

Science News for Kids: Echoes of Hunting
www.sciencenewsforkids.org/articles/20060426/Feature1.asp
For information on how bats use echolocation

INDEX

ABOUT THE AUTHOR

Susan H. Gray has a master's degree in zoology. She has written more than 70 science and reference books for children and especially loves writing about animals. Gray also likes to garden and play the piano. She lives in Cabot, Arkansas, with her husband, Michael, and many pets.